GU01019123

Not Cast Away.

Not Cast Away

by

Joy Fox

AVON BOOKS
AUBREY HOUSE, 83/85, BRIDGE ROAD
EAST MOLESEY, SURREY KT8 9HH

Printed and bound in the U.K.
Avon Books
London
First published 1993
© Joy Fox 1993
ISBN 1 897960 10 7

FOREWORD

Recently, reading a number of testimonies of Jews who have found Jesus Christ to be the Jewish Messiah, I have been amazed at the misconceptions they have previously had about Him. Many did not even know that He was Jewish, as were all the early disciples and apostles who constituted the Christian church.

But I found I also had misconceptions, imagining all synagogue-attending Jews to be well versed in Old Testament scriptures. Though why I should have thought so I don't know, as I know there are many who attend Christian services and have anything but a good knowledge of the Bible.

I also had the illusion that all evangelical Christians looked for the restoration of the nation of Israel in the land promised to their forefathers, and would have rejoiced to see God fulfil His promise made to Abraham thousands of years ago.

It was quite recently I discovered the editor of a Christian missionary magazine does not believe that God has a favourite people or a favourite land, and that Abraham in fact inherited the world; and that there are many more who hold this opinion.

I know that Christians differ in the interpretation of prophecy, and that these differences do not affect the personal salvation of those who have surrendered their lives to Christ, and trust in Him alone to save them.

At the same time my mind cannot comprehend how they can ignore such a mountain of evidence to the present day fulfilment of so much of scripture. There were times when I felt like quoting all the Bible and just saying 'Read it for yourself. But don't read it in little snippets here and there.

Read it through several chapters at a time and then read it again - and again.'

If your church substituted the works of Shakespeare for the Bible, and on the first Sunday, the reading was ten verses from Macbeth; the next, twelve verses from The Tempest; followed each Sunday by some verses from The Taming of the Shrew; then Hamlet; how long would it take until you could say you knew and understood the Shakespeare plays and what they were about?

I would say you never could, until you read each one through from start to finish. But how many read the books of the Bible from start to finish?

I gave my life to Jesus a life-time ago when I was seventeen and the first evidence of His work in my life was that I became an avid reader of the Bible. It was from reading the Bible alone that I have come to the opinions set out in what follows.

I came to share God's love for His special people, a love which never faltered through all their stiff-necked rejection of Him. 'Every one that loveth Him that begat, Loveth him also that is begotten of Him' (1 John 5:1) Punish them He did, for as Revelation, chapter 3 verse 19, states, 'As many as I love I rebuke and chasten'. But also, Malachi, chapter 3 verse 6, states, 'I am the Lord, I change not'. So how could He permanently turn His back on those He had loved and above all, break His promises to Abraham, Isaac and Jacob, who remained faithful to death and died believing the promises, 'having seen them afar off'; and one of the promises was that their seed would possess the Land 'for an everlasting possession.' (Genesis 17:8; 48:4)

Psalm 105, verses 6 to 11, puts it in a nutshell: 'O ye seed of Abraham His servant, ye children of Jacob His chosen.

He is the Lord our God. His judgements are in all the earth. He hath remembered His covenant for ever; the word which He commanded to a thousand generations. Which covenant He made with Abraham and His oath unto Isaac; and confirmed the same unto Jacob for an everlasting covenant, saying Unto thee will I give the Land of Canaan, the lot of your inheritance.'

Psalm 33 v. 11 states 'The counsel of the Lord standeth for ever, the thoughts of His heart to all generations'.

Psalm 119 v. 89 - 'For ever, O Lord, Thy Word is settled in Heaven.'

However we may differ, we can put our hope in God's word in Psalm 146 v. 8: 'The Lord openeth the eyes of the blind.' Those who come to Him asking to see, will see.

Note: All Bible references are taken from the Authorised Version, and Revised Version.

CHAPTER I

'God hath not cast away His people which He foreknew.' (Romans 11:2)

What a wonder it is to realize, those of us who love the Lord, that our names were being spoken before the world or the universe were created. So God's Word tells us. 'He hath chosen us in Him before the foundation of the World.' (Ephesians 1:4). So that when we discuss God's plan to create for Himself a people for His own possession (Titus 2:14), we do not begin at the beginning as is usual. We begin before the beginning.

Living outside of time and space, and knowing all things, the end as well as the beginning, God knew that this world which He was going to create would be a fallen world because of people's disbelief and disobedience to Him. So the plans He laid took account of the great cost to Himself of providing a way of escape from the penalty of disobedience, which is death.

God could have created for Himself robot figures, mechanically programmed to obey, but His desire was for a people who would freely love Him in return for the love he was going to pour on them. It is the nature of love to want to share, to give, to please and be loved in return. How can one love or be loved by a robot?

The created being had to partake in a measure of the nature and likeness of God and be free to choose His way for the choice to be of value. To be answerable we must have choice. So God determined to make man in His own image, give him the gift of free will, and with it, responsibility for his actions.

1

There would be a high price for man to pay for choosing his own way in opposition to God's way, and that price was death and eternal separation from Him. God foreknew that all would sin and come short of His glory (Romans 3:23), and that the sentence of death would have to be passed on all men.

How could men pay such a price and have fellowship with God? The only answer was for Someone to pay the price on man's behalf, to die in his stead, and offer the substitutionary benefits of His death to all who would confess their offences and believe their sins forgiven for His sake.

God could not just forgive disobedience, as this would be to condone rebellion, allowing man to go on sinning and being forgiven, with no change of heart or character. As a holy God, He could not bear the presence, the ugliness and hatefulness of sin. Justice demanded that the sentence of death had to be passed.

And with it, God's plan of redemption was laid and our names were being named. 'I will elect a man,' said God, 'and make of him a nation. I will reveal My nature and My laws for living to the nation through My servants the prophets. I will show them how I will redeem them from their sin by sending My only-begotten Son to be their Messiah and to die in their stead; in signs at first, so that they will recognize Him when He comes down among them. And My Will is that they will be a righteous nation, and a witness to the world of My redemption; that they will teach all the nations of the world how to know Me.'

'Behold, I have taught you statutes and judgements, even as the Lord my God commanded me, that ye should do so in the land whither ye go to possess it. Keep therefore and do them; for this is your wisdom and your understanding in the sight of the nations, which shall hear all these statutes, and say, Surely this great nation is a wise and understanding people. For what nation is there so great, who hath God so nigh unto them as the Lord our God is in all things that we call upon Him for? And what nation is there so great, that hath statutes and judgements so righteous as all this law, which I set before you this day?' (Deuteronomy 4:4-8). So spoke Moses, the greatest of the prophets.

From what God has revealed of His nature in His Word, I have no doubt at all that He would have desired that there never should be a fall. Ezekiel tells us in chapter 33 verse 11, 'As I live, saith the Lord God, I have no pleasure in the death of the wicked, but that the wicked turn from his way and live'. Paul tells Timothy in 1 Timothy chapter 2 verse 4 that, 'God our Saviour willeth that all men should be saved and come to the knowledge of the truth'.

But the Creator knew that what He would have desired and what would be were poles apart. Nevertheless, such was His love that He determined to create, and so the world and universe came into being, with animals, fish, birds and every green herb, and finally man, created in God's own image. Differing from the animal world, Adam and his help-meet Eve were created not only flesh and blood, but, by the breath of God, created living souls. They were aware of a spiritual world and had fellowship with their creator God.

Here it has to be said that God had an enemy - the prince of the power of the air (Ephesians 2:2). he created a beautiful being, an archangel, whose pride in his beauty and power caused him to rebel, and to aspire to receiving all the worship given to God the Creator. Anything created was a legitimate target to be destroyed by him; not always by outright violence, but often by subtlety and deception.

He was named Satan, and here was his opportunity to

strike a blow to the heart of a loving Creator, who had provided all that was necessary for His creatures' happiness in a perfect world where there was no necessity for the shedding of blood, no nature 'red in tooth and claw'. Only one restriction impinged on Adam and Eve's freedom, in order that they could of their own free will obey.

By hinting to the woman that God was withholding some good thing from her, Satan tempted her to disobey God's one restriction. Having become Satan's tool, she could be safely left to tempt Adam, and so the whole sorry story of sin entered the world, and the seed of sin was sown in every human born of Adam and Eve. The earth was cursed for man's sake, and from then on death and pain came about, where before they had not existed.

But God's purpose in creation was not to be thwarted. Right away when sin had entered the world, He revealed that the seed of the woman would bruise Satan's head. And the first blood was shed when 'the Lord God made coats of skins and clothed the man and the woman', who before this had no experience of shame in being naked. From then on, the shedding of animals' blood was to symbolize the death of the One Who was to pay the price to redeem man and restore the broken relationship between God and man.

Straightaway there was further disobedience. Adam and Eve had two sons, Cain and Abel. Cain was a farmer, tilling the ground and raising crops, while Abel kept sheep. When it came time to present an offering to God, Cain thought he could chose himself how to worship, and brought the first-fruits of his crops, while Abel brought the firstling of his sheep.

We are not told in what way God showed His displeasure by not accepting Cain's offering, while He accepted Abel's sacrifice of the lamb. But, in whatever way, it was apparent to Cain, who was so jealous of his brother that he murdered him.

Like every murderer and sinner from that day to this, he thought he could hide from God his evil deed and never have to give an account of his actions. But all things are open to the eyes of Him with Whom we have to do, and we will all have to give an account to God, not only for deeds but for every idle word. (Matthew 12:36).

The modern idea that God will accept any worship is as old as Cain. Jesus Messiah condemned the religious leaders as 'ye hypocrites, well did Isaiah prophecy of you saying 'This people draweth near to Me with their mouth and honoureth Me with their lips but their heart is far from Me. But in vain they do worship Me, teaching for doctrines the commandments of men.' (Matthew 15:7-9).

He also said, 'Not every one that saith unto Me, Lord, Lord, shall enter into the Kingdom of Heaven, but he that doeth the will of My Father which is in Heaven. Many will say to Me, Lord, Lord, have we not in Thy Name done many wonderful works. Then will I profess unto them, I never knew you.' (Matthew 7:21-22).

Isaiah, chapter 1 verse 13, shows God's displeasure at insincere worship. 'Bring no more vain oblations; it is iniquity, even the solemn assembly. Your appointed feasts My soul hateth, and when ye spread forth your hands I will hide Mine eyes from you, yea when ye make many prayers I will not hear.'

The only true creator, God will only be worshipped in the way He has revealed in His Word, the Bible. For He did not just create the world, and men and women to people it, and then leave them to get on with living in their own way. He had a plan for holy living, and the redemption of mankind

5

from the power and penalty of sin, and no other plan by man would replace it.

CHAPTER II

The heart is deceitful above all things and desperately wicked, who can know it? (Jeremiah 17:9)

The heart of man being desperately wicked, there was a period in the history of creation when God repented Him that He had made man on the earth, and it grieved Him as His heart (Genesis 6:6) and He thought to destroy the earth. But considering that He had always known this creation plan would bring Him pain, He did not utterly destroy it.

One man, Noah, found grace in His sight, and so God revealed to Noah how he and his family could escape the coming flood which was to be His means of bringing retribution. Noah was to build an ark of gopher wood, and pitch it inside and outside to make it watertight.

And Noah believed God's word and obeyed, though he must have had to endure the derision and mockery of those around him. 'Fancy building a boat where there is no water to float it. He must be mad.' And because he believed and obeyed, there came a time when his faith was vindicated and he and his family escaped the flood.

There can be no doubt that Noah explained what he was doing and why. If any others had believed, there would have been an opportunity for them to build their own ark and be saved as well. Their unbelief was the reason they perished. When the flood receded, God made a covenant promise between himself and the survivors that He would never again destroy the earth by a flood, a promise we remember when we see a rainbow!

Noah's family increased to repopulate the world. Again

sin and pride reared their ugly heads. Men decided to build a tower which would reach to heaven, as though heaven could be reached by any physical way devised by man. Any more than heaven can be disproved because man cannot reach it physically. Like the first astronaut sent into space by Russia, who made a derisory remark that he had not encountered God there.

It is so true that the Bible shows the heart of man has never changed, nor his foolishness in thinking that in his little sphere he can pit himself against the great Creator of the universe. What are a few hundred or thousand miles up in space when compared with the universe? The cosmonaut would have found God had he sought Him on earth.

To get back to Noah's descendants, we are told that God, knowing the wicked imaginations of their hearts, scattered them abroad in the earth, confounding their common language. So it is obvious their building of the tower was not an effort to find God and worship Him, but to challenge Him. They had started to build a city and this became the proto-type of rebellion against God. Babylon came into being.

Civilizations came into existence where men had used intellectual powers to make life comfortable in beautiful buildings and surroundings, but they were idolatrous and ignorant of spiritual truths about the nature of God; cruel in their worship and dealings with the weak and vulnerable in society. Children were burnt alive as sacrifices to their idols, wild orgies and feasts constituted worship.

Regarding God's testing of Abraham by calling on him, at a later date to offer up his son Isaac as a sacrifice, I have wondered if the sight of parents sacrificing their children to heathen deities had made Abraham doubtful if his love for the true God was so great.

It is certain that the testing was a witness to the world of the greatest of all sacrifices, when God watched His only Son die; when there could be no 'substitute' found, as in the case of Abraham, when there was a ram caught in a thicket.

But I believe it was also a self-revelation to Abraham, that his love and obedience could match the mistaken heathen worship of false gods. And it was upon such love and faith that the nation of Israel was founded.

CHAPTER III

Now the Lord had spoken to Abram, 'Get thee out of thy country ..... into a land that I will show thee.' (Genesis 12:1)

And the Lord said unto Abram ....'Lift up now thine eyes and look from the place where thou art northward and southward, eastward and westward - 'For all the land which thou seest, to thee will I give it and to thy seed forever.' (Genesis 13:14-15)

It was out of a heathen civilization that God spoke to Abram, calling him to leave the idolatrous city of Ur where he lived, and to go out not knowing where, but trusting God to lead him.

When Abram believed and obeyed, God made him some wonderful promises. Although he was childless, his name would be changed to Abraham (Genesis 17:5). He would become a father of nations, and his seed would be as the stars for number. God also gave him the land to which he had been led as an everlasting possession and promised that in Him all the families of the earth would be blessed.

And in this last promise we see the purpose of God in choosing Abraham. It was the Creator's will that the world as a whole would find blessing.

This covenant between God and Abraham was to be established through Isaac, the son of Abraham's wife Sarah, and not through Ishmael, the son of Sarah's bond-servant Hagar (Genesis 17:21). God also promised blessing to Ishmael (Genesis 21:13), but He had said, 'In Isaac shall thy seed be called' (Genesis 21:12).

When God renewed His covenant with Isaac (Genesis 26:3-5), again there was the promise of the land. 'Because that Abraham obeyed My voice and kept My charge, My commandments, My statutes and My laws'. Abraham being then dead, there never came a time when Abraham disobeyed. So God's promise was binding for all time.

When Isaac's wife Rebekah gave birth to twins, God revealed that the elder would serve the younger (Genesis 25:23). Esau was first-born, but the covenant promises fell on Jacob and we know Esau despised the birthright, ready to trade it for a 'mess of pottage' when he was hungry. (Genesis 25:29-34).

I feel I must say a word in support of Jacob, whose name means 'supplanter', as many think of him as a cheat and a trickster. After all, he was a twin brother of Esau, born practically at the same moment (Genesis 25:26). We must remember that Rebekah his mother had enquired of the Lord why 'the children struggled together within her'. The Lord told her two nations were in her womb and the elder should serve the younger.

It was Rebekah who told Jacob to seek the blessing of the first-born and who connived at deceiving Isaac. She was not the first one to try to bring about God's promise in her own way. Had not Sarah lost faith in being able to bear a son, and given her hand-maid to Abraham, resulting in the birth of Ishmael?

Without exception people see Jacob's sojourn with Laban as a time of cheating, and have not looked closely at the character of Laban.

We first meet Laban when Abraham sent his Servant, who ruled over all his household, to seek a wife for his son Isaac from among his own kindred. We have the wonderful

11

story in Genesis, chapter 24, of how the Lord guided the servant in finding Rebekah, and we are told 'Rebekah had a brother whose name was Laban'. Verse 30 tells us, 'And it came to pass when he saw the earrings and bracelets upon his sister's hands... he said, 'Come in thou blessed of the Lord' to the servant!

Later when Jacob was sent by his mother to Laban to escape the wrath of Esau, at being cheated of the birthright blessing, he fell in love with Laban's younger daughter Rachel and arranged with Laban to serve seven years for her hand in marriage (Genesis 29). We are told Jacob served seven years for Rachel, and they seemed unto him but a few days, for the love he had to her'.

It was Laban who was the cheat here, for when it came time to give Rachel as Jacob's wife, he gave him her elder sister Leah instead. It was too good a thing to lose a hired help and Jacob had to serve another seven years for Rachel.

When eleven of Jacob's twelve sons had been born, Jacob asked Laban to let him leave with his wives and children. But Laban had to admit, 'I have learned by experience that the Lord hath blessed me for thy sake' (Genesis 30:27). As Jacob said, 'It was little which thou hadst before I came and it is now increased into a multitude and the Lord hath blessed thee since my coming and now when shall I provide for mine own house also?' Not much cheating there by Jacob!

To obtain wages from Laban he used methods to increase his own animal stock, but this enraged Laban who was not content that his own stock had greatly increased under Jacob's care. And we are told in Genesis chapter 31 that Jacob confided to his wives Leah and Rachel, 'Ye know that with all my power I have served your father. And your father hath deceived me and changed my wages ten times. But God suffered him not to hurt me.'

Rachel and Leah testified against their father Laban, 'Are we not counted of him strangers? For he hath sold us and hath quite devoured also our money.'

Jacob then left, to return with all his family and cattle to his father Isaac, and Laban pursued in anger, though warned by God in a dream not to harm Jacob. We have in chapter 31 Jacob's own account to confront Laban with. 'This twenty years have I been with thee; thy ewes and thy she-goats have not cast their young and the rams of the flock have I not eaten. That which was torn of beasts I brought not to thee; I bare the loss of it; of my hand thou didst require it whether stolen by day or stolen by night. Thus was I in the day the drought consumed me and the frost by night and my sleep departed from mine eyes. Thus have I been twenty years in thy house. I served thee fourteen years for thy two daughters and six years for thy cattle and thou hast changed my wages ten times.' Note well, this was not to increase by yearly increments!

As Jacob said, 'Except the God of my Fathers, the God of Abraham and the fear of Isaac had been with me, surely thou hadst sent me away now empty. God hath seen mine affliction and the labour of my hands and rebuked thee.'

Where have people got the idea that Jacob was a born cheat just because he followed his mother's advice to obtain the blessing of the first-born and to be the inheritor of the covenant? Jacob had what we now call "stickability"; entirely lacking in Esau. And Laban was what we would call an old skinflint.

To Jacob God gave the name Israel and confirmed the covenant which He had made with Abraham and Isaac, promising the Land (Genesis 32:28; 35:10,12). As Hebrews ch. 11 v. 13 tells us, 'These all died in faith, not having received the promises but having seen them afar off'. If God has

13

changed His mind about the land, then they believed a lie. But we have to consider the character of the God Who made the promises. In Numbers chapter 23 verse 19 we are told, 'God is not a man that He should lie; neither the son of man that He should repent. Hath He said and shall He not do it? Or hath He spoken and shall He not make it good?'

We read in Exodus, chapter 34 verse 6, 'And the Lord passed by before him (Moses) and proclaimed 'The Lord, the Lord God, merciful and gracious, longsuffering and abundant in goodness and truth.' Moses himself testified (Deuteronomy 4:31), 'For the Lord thy God is a merciful God. He will not forsake thee, neither destroy thee, nor forget the covenant of thy Fathers which He sware unto them.'

Malachi, in chapter 3 verses 5/6, states, 'I will come near to you to judgement and I will be a swift witness against the sorcerers and against the adulterers and against false swearers, and against those that oppress the hireling in his wages, the widow and the fatherless, and turn aside the stranger from his right, and fear not Me, saith the Lord of Hosts, for I am the Lord, I change not.'.

We are building our faith, and the covenant is built, on solid rock, when we trust the Lord to keep His promises. And we will see from the last scripture that God does not just expect our worship but He expects us to behave in a manner which pleases Him in our everyday lives - to bear, as it were, a family resemblance to Him as our Heavenly Father.

CHAPTER IV

And I will bring you into the Land concerning which I sware to give it to Abraham..... and I will give it to you for a heritage. (Exodus 6:8)

So, taking a bird's eye view of the history of Israel, we come to the point where Abraham's seed, through Isaac and Jacob become a nation, though a nation in bondage in Egypt, as had been shewn to Abraham in a dream. (Genesis 15:12-21). God heard their distress and prepared Moses to lead His people from bondage into the Land of promise.

Moses had been one of the Hebrew boy children whom Pharaoh had decreed must be put to death. His mother had placed him in a little cradle in the river as though there was an attempt to obey the decree. But she had left Moses' sister Miriam to watch what would happen to him.

As it turned out, it was God's decree that Moses should live. Pharaoh's daughter heard the baby crying and told her maids to bring him to her. She loved the child and decided to bring him up as her own son. Not only did Moses live, but Miriam said she could get a nurse for him, and of course brought their own mother, who was then engaged to look after her own baby.

Moses, being brought up as an Egyptian prince, was educated to the highest standard. And having his own mother as nursemaid, he was made aware of his origins and hated to see his Hebrew people oppressed. In defending one of the slaves against ill-treatment, he killed an Egyptian task-master, and when it became known, had to flee the country.

When Moses arrived in Midian, he stopped by a well.

The Bible story continues: 'Now the priest of Midian had seven daughters and they came and drew water and filled the trough to water their father's flock. And the shepherds came and drove them away, but Moses stood up and helped them (the daughters of course), and watered their flock. And when they came to Reuel their father he said, 'How is it that ye are come so soon today?' And they said, 'An Egyptian delivered us out of the hand of the shepherds and also drew water enough for us and watered the flock.' And he said unto his daughters 'And where is he? Why is it that ye have left the man? Call him that he may eat bread.' And Moses was content to dwell with the man and he gave Moses Zipporah his daughter.'

No wonder the Bible describes Moses as meek above all the men on earth. And meekness is not weakness. He was able to drive off a number of bullying shepherds. And the task God had elected him to carry out was not suitable for a weak man.

Moses enjoyed his quiet life for forty years before his peace was shattered. God's time had come to deliver Israel from bondage. The Pharaoh who had sought Moses' life was dead, so Moses would not be recognized when he returned to Egypt.

God's call, from the bush which seemed to be burning, found a very unwilling conscript; so unwilling that God allowed his brother Aaron to be his spokesman, and to accompany him as he returned to Egypt, to confront Pharaoh with God's demand - 'Let My people go.' (Exodus 5;1).

It took ten plagues on the Egyptians before they would let their servants and slaves go, and it was the last one, when all the first-born in the land died, which persuaded Pharaoh at last to give in.

God had always placed a difference between the

16

Egyptians and His Hebrew people. The Hebrews were to slay a lamb without blemish and sprinkle the blood on the door-posts of their houses and the destroying angel would pass over their homes. They were to roast the lamb and eat it with unleavened bread and bitter herbs, in haste and ready to set out on a journey.

And the great deliverance came when they left Egypt in their thousands and set out to enter the land which God had promised to them; a land flowing with milk and honey. No more task-masters standing over them with lash and whip forcing them to make bricks. They were free. God's presence was continually with them, being apparent before them as a pillar of cloud by day, and a pillar of fire from behind by night.

Pharaoh soon rued his decision to let these slaves go and followed with his chariots and horsemen. All he had seen of God's power had not persuaded him. But neither had it persuaded the Hebrews, who were terrified when they saw they were between the army and the sea and they could see no way they could escape.

Again Jehovah demonstrated His power, causing a great wind to push back the sea allowing the Hebrews to cross over on dry land. Just as they had all passed over, the Egyptians had reached the sea and thought they could pursue on dry land too, but the wind died down and the water came crashing down on them and all were drowned.

This great deliverance from the bondage of Egypt was commanded by God to be commemorated yearly, reminding the Hebrews and their children to come, of God's great power and His love for His people. It would also demonstrate how Jehovah would redeem His people from the slavery of sin and lead them to freedom and restored fellowship with Himself. The Lamb slain, without blemish and a firstling of the flock, was a type of the one true sacrifice of the Lamb of God which taketh away the sin of the world - Jesus, their Messiah.

It is not to be supposed that it was a grateful people who were redeemed from bondage. From the beginning they were a grumbling, murmuring, and disobedient people. God had to say of them: 'They are quickly turned out of the way which I commanded them - they have made them a molten image.' (Deuteronomy 9:12).

Moses' experience of them was, 'Ye have been rebellious against the Lord from the day that I knew you.' (Deuteronomy 9:24) And it was because of this rebellion that Moses was not allowed to lead them into the Land of promise straight away. God made them wander forty years in the wilderness and the desert, until the older generation, whose hearts hankered after the gods of Egypt, had died.

The people had refused to go in and conquer the land, believing the men whom Moses had sent in to spy out the land, who thought the inhabitants were too strong to be overcome. If only they had believed Joshua and Caleb, who tried to persuade them they were well able to take the land, what a different history there would have been.

Later, after Moses died and God had elected Joshua in his stead, Joshua also sent two spies before entering the land. They lodged at Rahab's house on the walls of Jericho. Rahab showed that though the people may have appeared strong and hard to overcome, they were in fact a demoralized people. Rahab says, 'I know that the Lord hath given you the land and that your terror is fallen upon us and that all the inhabitants of the land faint because of you. For we have heard how the Lord dried up the water of the Red Sea for you when you came out of Egypt, and what ye did to the two kings of the Amorites that were on the other side of Jordan, whom ye utterly destroyed. And as soon as we had heard these things our hearts did melt neither did there remain any more courage in any man because of you.' (Joshua 2:9-11; Deuteronomy 28:10).

If they had been obedient and believing, Israel would have been spared forty years of wandering in the wilderness, and Moses would have been able to lead them into the promised land, and establish them in right worship and living. As Isaiah states in chapter 48 verse 18, 'O that thou hadst hearkened to My commandments; then had thy peace been as a river and thy righteousness as the waves of the sea.'

CHAPTER V

The Lord hath avouched thee this day to be His peculiar people, that thou shouldest keep all His commandments that thou mayest be a holy people unto the Lord thy God. (Deuteronomy 26:18-19)

There are those who believe it was not fair that nations should be cast out to allow Israel to occupy the land. Though as Creator, the land belonged to God and He referred to it as 'My land' (Jeremiah 16:18) and it is obvious He could give it to whom He would, it must not be supposed that it was an innocent people who were dispossessed.

Leviticus chapter 18 details the sins of those people, and in verse 25 the Lord states, 'The land is defiled, therefore I do visit the iniquity thereof upon it and the land itself vomiteth out her inhabitants.' We are told in Deuteronomy, chapter 12 verse 31, 'Every abomination to the Lord which He hateth have they done unto their gods, for even their sons and their daughters they have burnt in the fire to their gods.'

From modern knowledge of such decadent living, the inhabitants must have been riddled with disease. (See Deuteronomy 7:15; 28:27-28).

It was because of abominations that the Lord cast out the inhabitants of the land before Israel.

Moses made it clear that it was not because Israel were righteous. 'Speak not thou in thine heart that the Lord thy God hath cast them out from before thee saying 'For my righteousness the Lord hath brought me in to possess the land.' But for the wickedness of those nations the Lord doth drive them out before thee. Not for thy righteousness but for the wickedness of those nations. Understand therefore that the Lord thy God giveth thee not this land to possess it for thy righteousness; for thou art a stiff-necked people.' (Deuteronomy 9:4-6).

And so, after wandering forty years in the wilderness, Israel was brought at last to enter the land chosen by God, and promised as an everlasting possession - not led by Moses, who was only permitted by God to view the land, but not to enter it. God chose Joshua to lead His people into their inheritance.

From the beginning, although they had been warned not to enquire after the gods of the inhabitants of the land (Deuteronomy 12:30) they were disobedient, and idolatry crept into their worship. Under wise Judges, there were periods of peace, until Samuel, the last and greatest of the Judges.

Always wanting to be like the other nations, they began to desire a king to rule over them, and God allowed Samuel to give them a king. Saul was by outward appearance tall and handsome, but, as it turned out, weak and undisciplined. And because of Saul's disobedience God rejected him from starting a royal line.

Although Saul's son Jonathan was faithful and true to the Lord, to have had him become king would have been the delight of Saul's heart, and God could not allow that.

It is likely that God had already intended that Israel should have a king and would have brought David to occupy the throne in His own time. 'And the Lord said unto Samuel, How long wilt thou mourn for Saul, seeing I have rejected him from reigning over Israel? Fill thine horn with oil, and go, I will send thee to Jesse the Bethlehemite; for I have provided Me a king among his sons.' (1 Samuel 16:1).

David came to represent all that was best in kingship and obedience to God; ready to repent sincerely when he sinned, and to seek God's guidance in ruling his people - a man after God's own heart (1 Samuel 13:14). So much so that God promised his throne would be established for ever (2 Samuel 7:16) and that the Messiah would come of his seed. (Jeremiah 23:5-6; Acts 2:29-30; 13:23).

What a different world it would have been if this nation had become a willing instrument in the hands of God to carry out His will. But their history makes sad reading. Even the son of David, the wise Solomon who began well, in later life turned away after strange gods just to indulge his many wives and concubines. (1 Kings ch. 11). It was under Solomon's foolish son Rehoboam that the nation was divided. All the tribes except Judah and Benjamin broke away, making Jeroboam their king, and formed the northern kingdom of Israel in opposition to Judah. Jeroboam, to establish his kingdom, and to prevent his people from going to Jerusalem for the religious festivals, and perhaps returning to accept David's line in the kingdom of Judah, worked out his own religious plans, making idols to be worshipped, and ordaining feasts and festivals, and a new priesthood in opposition to God's ordained Levites.

There was no way God could overlook the rebellion of His chosen people, though He time and again forgave them and called them to change their ways. There were periods when, under the influence of godly kings they returned to following the Lord, but frequently they had evil kings, who led them to commit even worse abominations than the nations whom the Lord had cast out of the land before them.

Jeremiah tells us 'The children of Judah have done evil in My sight, saith the Lord, they have set their abominations in the House which is called by My Name, to pollute it. They have built the High Places to burn their sons and their daughters in the fire, which I commanded not, neither came it into My heart.' (Jeremiah 7:30-31).

Ezekiel speaks of Jerusalem: 'Wilt thou judge the bloody city? Yes, Thou shalt show her all her abominations.' 'Thou hast despised My holy things and hast profaned My Sabbaths. In thee are men that carry tales to shed blood; in the midst of thee is lewdness.' (Ezekiel 22:2 & 8-9).

In chapter 16 He states, 'Thou hast taken thy sons and thy daughters whom thou hast borne unto Me and these hast thou sacrificed unto them to be devoured. Is this of thy whoredoms a small matter? That thou hast slain My children and delivered them to cause them to pass through the fire?' (verses 20-21)

In the end, sin bore its own fruit. They were what God called a stiff-necked people who persecuted and slew God's messengers to them (Jeremiah 2:30) until there was no remedy other than to dispossess them of the land.

The Northern kingdom of Israel was first overcome and taken captive by the King of Assyria, to be scattered out of existence (2 Kings 17).

It was not long before the kingdom of Judah was also overcome, and the people carried off to Babylon, having ignored all the words of the Lord through Jeremiah. But still God was gracious to them, promising that at the end of seventy years He would bring them back to their own land.

Always when Israel as a nation was failing to obey the Lord, He had His remnant of faithful people. When Elijah the prophet was very discouraged, saying, 'I have been very jealous for the Lord God of Hosts, because the children of Israel have forsaken Thy covenant, thrown down Thine altars and slain Thy prophets with the sword, and I, even I only, am left, and they seek my life to take it way.' (1 Kings 19:10,14). God's reply, to encourage him, was, (v.18) 'Yet I have left Me seven thousand in Israel all the knees which have not bowed unto Baal and every mouth which hath not kissed him.'

Perhaps each of those seven thousand thought he or she was the only one not worshipping Baal, but the Lord knew His own, and His purpose would be fulfilled through them.

God continued to raise up prophets and reveal to them His Word. Even when the nation had been carried off to Babylon He spoke to His people through Daniel and Ezekiel.

His continued purpose in speaking through the prophets was to reveal His plan for the redemption of mankind from the penalty of sin and His plans for the nations, particularly His covenant people Israel. The prophets foretold the coming of Messiah, sometimes as the suffering Servant, as in Isaiah chapter 53; sometimes looking further forward to His coming as King to reign in Zion (Micah 5:2).

Following the captivity in Babylon, the history of the nation was such that never again did they have political independence except for a short period under the Maccabees. After seventy years in Babylon, some were given permission to return to Jerusalem and build the Temple, but not freedom to set up an independent kingdom.

In fact, such was their suffering under a succession of overlords that their one longing was for Messiah to come as a conquering king to destroy their enemies. They persuaded themselves that the nation was the suffering servant and so missed recognizing Messiah Jesus when He came to be born in a stable of humble parents.

But still there were the few whose eyes God opened to the truth. Those who faithfully awaited the coming Messiah. As has already been said, the Feast of Passover instituted by Moses was not merely a remembrance of God's deliverance

24

of His people from slavery in Egypt, but was in token of His redemption from the slavery of sin. John the Baptist recognized this when he pointed to Jesus as 'the Lamb of God Which taketh away the sin of the world.'

Jesus pointed out to the two disciples on the road to Emmaus to whom He appeared after His resurrection, 'Ought not Christ to have suffered these things?.... and, beginning at Moses and all the prophets, He expounded unto them in all the scriptures the things concerning Himself' (Luke 24:26-27). So much for those who say we can do without the Old Testament. God knew there had to be a remedy for sin before there could be victory in living.

And so the climax of the nation's rejection of God was the great tragedy and sin of their rejection of their Messiah. The religious leaders 'searched the scriptures' constantly and yet they did not recognize Him though He was there to be recognized. 'They testify of Me' He said in John ch. 5 v.39. 'He came to His own but His own received Him not'. (John 1:11).

In the pride of their hearts they were set to establish their own righteousness (Romans 10:3; Matthew 6:1-5). They would not accept the poverty of that righteousness before a holy God. And the fact that this carpenter's son should speak with such authority infuriated them. (Matthew 7:29).

It must be known that long before our Lord came to earth, the Jewish religious leaders did not only hold with the divine authority of the books of the Old Testament, but had built up writings and interpretations in the Talmud which were revered above the writings of the prophets.

Jesus was referring to this when He accused the religious leaders of 'lading men with burdens grievous to be borne.' (Luke 11:46).

When Solomon's Temple was destroyed and the bulk of the nation taken captive to Babylon, there had to be a substitute for the animal sacrificing for sin enjoined in the books of Moses, and so there was built up a mountain of 'do's and don'ts' as a way of approaching God.

These were not abandoned when the new temple was built and the ritual of animal sacrifices resumed. In fact they have been continually added to, and even more so, since the overthrow of the nation by the Romans in AD 70, when the second temple and ritual were completely destroyed.

Rabbinic writings and leadership replaced the priestly functions. To try to rationalize the inability to carry out the sacrificial laws, and so the interpretation of these sacrifices as atonement for sin, the people came to believe that there was no need for an intermediary between man and God, nor a substitutionary sacrifice.

They believed - as many nominal Christians do - that men could approach God with good deeds, and accrue merits to present to Him. They had no conception of the holiness of God, nor of the sinfulness of man, nor of the great gulf which separates the two.

It seems incredible that God lived among them in the flesh, albeit in the form of a servant, yet they could not recognize holiness when they saw it, nor the voice of authority when they heard it. In fact they hated that holiness and authority which condemned their own self-love.

Their blindness was past believing, as testified by their assertion to Jesus that 'We be Abraham's seed and were never in bondage to any man,' (John 8:33) at a time when they were in subjection to Rome, and had been to numerous nations before that.

It was occupation of the Land which signified the

favour of Jehovah their God. Now that they had spurned and betrayed the Messiah, there was no other remedy than that God should dispossess them. From being protected, they became a prey to the great enemy of souls, and were scattered throughout the world, to suffer unspeakable persecutions down the years.

And what of the Remnant? These became the newly born Christian Church, totally Jewish, who fulfilled the promise made to Abraham so long before, that his seed would be a blessing to the world - first through Messiah and then through His disciples; and the promise that the Word of the Lord would go forth from Jerusalem. These early believers were also scattered, and took the gospel abroad with them, and so inevitably the gentiles came to believe.

That Christian gospel has been preached throughout the world, and no one can deny its Jewish origin, and that all believers have been blessed through the seed of Abraham.

And God has preserved His Jewish Remnant of believers as a distinct people and race. Though many thousands have assimilated with the nations to which they were scattered, there is a growing number of Messianic believers who are a blessing to the world and to their own nation of Israel, in spreading the good news of Yeshua Ha Meshiach.

CHAPTER VI

And the Lord shall inherit Judah His portion in the Holy Land and shall choose Jerusalem again. (Zechariah 2:12)

To many people in our generation the expulsion of the Jews from their land showed that God had totally rejected them as a nation, and as His chosen people. So again we must look to the faithfulness of the God Who made His covenant with Abraham, with Isaac, with Jacob, with Judah and with the nation.

Jeremiah tells us in chapter 31, verse 37, 'Thus saith the Lord, If heaven above can be measured, and the foundations of the earth searched out beneath, I will also cast off all the seed of Israel for all that they have done, saith the Lord'. Verse 38, 'Behold the days come saith the Lord, that the city shall be built to the Lord'. Verse 40, 'and the whole valley ... shall be holy unto the Lord. It shall not be plucked up nor thrown down any more for ever'.

Again Jeremiah declares in chapter 33 verses 24 to 26: 'Considerest thou not what this people have spoken saying, the two families which the Lord hath chosen He hath even cast them off? Thus have they despised My people that they should no more be a nation before them. Thus saith the Lord, If My covenant be not with day and night and if I have not appointed the ordinances of heaven and earth, then will I cast away the seed of Jacob and David My servant ... for I will cause their captivity to return and have mercy on them.'

Psalm 89 verses 29 to 34 states, 'His seed also will I make to endure for ever. If his children forsake My law, and keep not My commandments, then will I visit with the rod. Nevertheless My loving-kindness will I not utterly take from him, nor suffer My faithfulness to fail. My covenant will I not break nor alter the thing that is gone out of My lips.'

These are only a sample of many such declarations which make it obvious that if God can break His Word to Israel, then He can break His Word to the church. Such a thing is unthinkable.

There are those who interpret the New Covenant foretold in Jeremiah (chapter 31 verse 31) as having been meant for the Christian church. But God's word state clearly this is promised to the 'House of Judah' and refers back to the day He brought them out of the land of Egypt, and of their breaking the first covenant. This could never refer to the church.

The church certainly partakes of the blessings of the New Covenant. Ephesians (3:6) shows 'that the Gentiles should be fellow heirs and of the same body, and partakers of His promise in Christ by the gospel.' Paul states, 'At that time ye were without Christ, being aliens from the commonwealth of Israel, and strangers from the covenants of promise, having no hope, and without God in the world. But now in Christ Jesus, ye who sometimes were far off, are made nigh by the blood of Christ. For He is our peace who hath made both one.' (Ephesians 2:12-14).

That does not say 'You Gentiles have replaced Israel and are the new heirs.' It says 'You share the promises in Christ with Israel.'

Those who hold replacement theology, believing the promises, which could never have any relevance to the Gentile church - especially regarding the dispersion and regathering to the Land - no longer apply to Israel, need to examine their hearts, for I believe they will discover their blind spot is anti-semitism. And there is only one who inspires such feelings and that is Satan, who seeks to blind their eyes to the truth, thereby depriving Israel of a great body of prayers for her restoration.

If in spite of Paul's warning and rebuke in Romans chapter 11 verses 18 to 21, they can boast themselves against the branches broken off, then they are resisting the Holy Spirit Who spoke through Paul.

Paul, in Romans chapter 11 verse 17, refers to the Gentile church as a wild olive tree grafted in to the original olive tree of Israel. And it must be pointed out that grafting takes place on a living plant, not a dead one. It is only branches which have been broken off and branches which have been grafted in. The church is no new olive tree, and Paul speaks of the restoration of the original branches. In chapter 3 verse 6 Paul writes, 'that the Gentiles should be fellow-heirs, and of the same body, and partakers of His promise in Christ by the gospel.' Note the words 'fellow-heirs.'

Those who claim that the church is the new Israel state that the many promises of restoration and the regathering of those who were sent into captivity were fulfilled following the seventy years in Babylon. In fact although a number returned to Jerusalem with the consent of Cyrus, Darius and Artaxerxes, yet they had to confess, 'Behold we are servants this day and for the land that Thou gavest unto our Fathers to eat the fruit thereof, and the good thereof, behold we are servants in it.' (Nehemiah 9:36).

They never had true sovereignty and freedom as a nation, except, as already stated, for a brief spell under the Maccabees. And no way could it be claimed that, following the return from Babylon, 'No more' would they be a prey to the heathen. Nor could it be claimed that the return from Babylon was in the 'latter days'.

Jesus, when foretelling the destruction of Jerusalem,

and the scattering of the nation into captivity, spoke of the times of the Gentiles (Luke 21:20-24) showing there was a limited time to the casting off of the nation. He also stated while weeping over Jerusalem, 'Ye shall not see Me henceforth till ye say 'Blessed is He that cometh in the Name of the Lord.' (Matthew 23:39).

So as they are going to see Him, for every eye shall see Him, they are going to say 'Blessed is He that cometh in the Name of the Lord'. Also, Paul states that 'blindness in part is happened to Israel until the fulness of the gentiles be come in.' (Romans 11:25).

We who live in the closing days of the twentieth century, see this Jewish people, who have been scattered throughout the world and persecuted in horrendous ways, now once again restored to the Land promised to their forefathers; once again speaking the language of Zion - in my youth counted among the 'dead' languages - but promised in Jeremiah, 'As yet they shall use this speech in the Land of Judah and in the cities thereof when I shall bring again their captivity'. (Jeremiah 31:23).

A few years ago it would have been inconceivable that Jews in communist countries would have had liberty to return to their Land, yet we see God's miracle before our eyes as the Iron Curtain has been pulled down, and now there are no restrictions on those who wish to leave, and they are flooding into Israel.

It seems quite clear that whether one reckons from 14th May 1948, when Israel declared her independence, or from 1967, during the Six Day War when the city of Jerusalem was unified, the times of the Gentiles have been fulfilled and Israel has come into her own.

From now on we can look to the Lord's word that 'I

will accept you with your sweet savour, when I bring you out from the people, and gather you out of the countries wherein ye have been scattered; and I will be sanctified in you before the heathen. And ye shall know that I AM the Lord, when I shall bring you into the Land of Israel, into the country for the which I lifted up Mine hand to give it to your Fathers. And there shall ye remember your ways, and all your doings wherein ye have been defiled, and ye shall loathe yourselves in your own sight for all your evils that ye have committed. And ye shall know that I Am the Lord when I have wrought with your for My Name's sake, not according to your wicked ways, nor according to your corrupt doings, O ye House of Israel, saith the Lord God. (Ezekiel 20:41-44).

The Jewish people have returned to the Land in unbelief but as the promises regarding their return have been fulfilled, so will the promises regarding their repentance and turning to the Lord be fulfilled. Note also that the nation is brought into the land before they repent.

CHAPTER VII

He hath remembered His covenant forever, the word which He commanded to a thousand generations. Which covenant He made with Abraham and His oath unto Isaac. And confirmed the same unto Jacob for a law and to Israel for an everlasting covenant. Saying 'Unto thee will I give the Land of Canaan, the lot of your inheritance.' (Psalm 105:8-11).

Although many evangelical Christians look for the restoration of Israel as a nation, once more serving the Lord and acknowledging Jesus as their Messiah, there are still many who are not persuaded. There are those who believe that God has no longer a favourite people or a favourite land.

To believe this they have to ignore large tracts of scripture. The return of the Jewish people to the promised land must be a great embarrassment to them. They have got to believe also that God no longer rules in the kingdom of men.

We are told in Daniel chapter 4, verses 17, 25, 32 & 35, that King Nebuchadnezzar's dream was 'to the intent that the living may know that the Most High ruleth in the kingdom of men, and giveth it to whomsoever He will.' Did then God make a mistake in allowing the Jewish homeland to be set up in Israel? Or was He impotent to stop it? Never. 'I change not' He declares. King Nebuchadnezzar learned to acknowledge that 'He doeth according to His will in the army of Heaven and among the inhabitants of the earth; and none can stay His hand or say to Him 'What doest Thou?'

How do these believers interpret many other scriptures? Hosea states in chapter 3, verses 4 & 5, 'For the children of Israel shall abide many days without a king and without a prince

33

and without sacrifice and without an image and without ephod and without teraphim. Afterward shall the children of Israel return and seek the Lord their God and David their King and shall fear the Lord and His goodness in the latter days'.

The Church may share many blessing with Israel, and be called the Israel of God, but it has never been called 'the Children of Israel'. Nor has it been involved with sacrifice and ephod etc.

Scripture is clear that where personal salvation is concerned there is no difference between circumcised and uncircumcised, Jew and Gentile, male and female (Romans 4:11; Galatians 3:28). There is not one means of salvation for one different from that of another. The blood of Jesus Christ is the only remedy for sin.

But God has plans for nations as well as individuals. Speaking through Ezekiel, He declares, 'I will set My glory among the nations and all the nations shall see My judgement that I have executed, and My hand that I have laid upon them. So the House of Israel shall know that I am the Lord their God from that day and forward. And the nations shall know that the House of Israel went into captivity for their iniquity' (Ezekiel 39:21-23). Verse 25 states, 'Therefore thus saith the Lord God; Now will I bring again the captivity of Jacob, and have mercy upon the whole House of Israel'.

God's promises continue; 'When I have brought them again from the peoples, and gathered them out of their enemies' lands, and am sanctified in them in the sight of many nations; then shall they know that I am the Lord their God, Which caused them to be led into captivity among the nations: but I have gathered them unto their own Land..... Neither will I hide My face any more from them: for I have poured out My Spirit upon the House of Israel, saith the Lord God.' (Verses 27-29).

No one can doubt this is a future prophecy. We have seen the nation gathered back to the Land but so far in unbelief. This could not refer to past captivity, for the promise 'Neither will I hide My face any more from them' could not have referred to the return from Babylon. God's face did in fact turn from them for their rejection of Messiah. Also, the promises are of restoration and forgiveness to a people who have sinned, and been scattered. These blessings could not be applicable to the Church.

We believe the promises because of the immutability of God's Covenant. Speaking through Moses, He shows what will befall the Nation for its disobedience, but states, 'And yet for all that, when they be in the land of their enemies, I will not cast them away, neither will I abhor them to destroy them utterly, and to break My Covenant with them: for I am the Lord their God. But I will for their sakes remember the Covenant of their ancestor, whom I brought forth out of the Land of Egypt in the sight of the heathen, that I might be their God: I am the Lord.' (Leviticus 26:44-45).

CHAPTER VIII

Wherefore do I see every man with his hands on his loins as a woman in travail and all faces are turned to paleness? Alas! for that day is great so that none is like it; it is even the time of Jacob's trouble. (Jeremiah 30:6-7).

There are those who believe that Israel has yet to go through a period of great suffering and that the time of Jacob's trouble has yet to be fulfilled.

It is my own belief that the description above of Jacob's trouble describes perfectly the Holocaust. The horrors of the concentration camps over a number of years will never be repeated, and unless God's intention were to wipe out the whole nation, never again will six million be exterminated in such ghastly circumstances.

Could any war exceed the horrors of the Holocaust? When people are fighting back and defending themselves, being killed is never so horrific as when, over a number of years, they are living in mortal fear of every knock on the door, of what news they will hear of loved ones taken away, of the horrors of the concentration camps, starvation, gas chambers. How can anyone say there is worse to come? Could there be anything worse?

Jeremiah would confirm this. He says, 'They that be slain with the sword are better than they that be slain with hunger; for these pine away, stricken through for want of the fruits of the field.' (Lamentations 4:9).

If, as I believe, the Times of the Gentiles has been fulfilled, never again will Israel be at the mercy of her enemies. Some will surely die when the nations are gathered together against her, but it is then that the Lord will make apparent His intervention on her behalf, and He will be sanctified in her in the eyes of the nations of the world.

Isaiah says, in chapter 51 verse 17, 'Awake awake, stand up, O Jerusalem, which hast drunk at the hand of the Lord the cup of His fury; thou hast drunken the dregs of the cup of trembling and wrung them out.' Verse 21: 'Therefore hear now this thou afflicted and drunken but not with wine.' Verse 22: 'Thus saith thy Lord, the Lord and thy God, that pleadeth the cause of His people, Behold I have taken out of thy hand the cup of trembling, even the dregs of the cup of My fury; thou shalt no more drink of it again.'

I believe the return to the Land marks the turning point. Scripture after Scripture, referring to the latterday return to the Land, indicate that 'NO MORE' will Israel be under the yoke of her enemies and 'NO More' will God forsake her though she has as yet not acknowledged her Messiah.

Ezekiel, chapters 38 and 39, seems to indicate that she will not recognize her Lord until all the nations have gathered together against her. Only then will she realize that she has not overcome on her own, but that God has destroyed her enemies.

Even the nations will recognize the supernatural nature of the defence of Israel. I believe that this will be through a great earthquake, greater than any yet experienced on earth, (Ezekiel 38:19; Revelation 16:18), rather than by military means, though it could be originated by an atomic bomb.

'Surely in that day there shall be a great shaking in the land of Israel so that the fishes of the sea and the fowls of the heaven and the beasts of the field... and all the men that are upon the face of the earth shall shake at My presence and the mountains shall be thrown down and the steep places shall fall and every wall shall fall to the ground... and I will rain upon him (Gog) and upon his bands and upon the many people that are with him, an overflowing rain and great hailstones, fire and brimstone.... And I will be known in the eyes of many nations. (Ezekiel 38:19-23).

I wonder if it will be at the same time that the waters of the Salt Sea will be 'healed'. The waters are salt because there is no outlet. It could be that the great earthquake will make a rift into the Mediterranean through which the waters of the lake would flow, and in a short time the Salt Sea would be 'sweet', and fish would be able to live in it.

'And it shall come to pass that the fishers shall stand upon it from En-gedi even unto En-eglaim; their fish shall be according to their kinds, as the fish of the great sea (the Mediterranean), exceeding many. But the mirey places thereof and the marshes thereof shall not be healed; they shall be given to salt.' (Ezekiel 47:10-11).

There is no need for Israel to look to other nations for weapons to help her fight her enemies when they gather to seek to destroy her. The Lord will.

CHAPTER IX

For the Lord hath chosen Jacob until Himself and Israel for His peculiar treasure. (Psalm 135:4).

There is a subject which has to be considered in God's choice of Israel as a nation to fulfil His purposes in His world; the question of the election of Israel in preference to the other nations.

Considering how often the nation failed to obey God and how often they rebelled and went after other gods, surely the wisdom of God in choosing them would be called in question, especially so as He knew all that would happen before the creation.

First of all, we must establish the fact that God is not only Sovereign, above all principalities and powers, but all wisdom, love, righteousness, justice, holiness, knowledge and power belong to Him. So what ought to be brought into question is not His wisdom but our assessment of it. Judging from the history of mankind in the Bible narrative, there is no doubt that any nation which was chosen would have failed.

And we must remember the choosing was not favouritism in the human sense, but Israel was chosen to be a holy people unto the Lord; to do a work in extending God's Kingdom among the nations of the world. And Deuteronomy, chapter 4 verse 37, tells us, 'Because He loved thy Fathers, therefore He chose their seed after them.'

As God had created the world, He has a supreme right like any master to choose to promote whom He will.

The thorny question of freedom and election must be faced. There are those who believe it is well nigh blasphemy to suggest that man has any part to play in his own spiritual destiny. God has elected some men and women to salvation, for reasons known only to God Himself. But as the whole world is doomed because of sin, if God chooses to elect some to salvation He is not being unjust, but generous.

But the Bible teaches that the offer of salvation was to all men. The angels who announced the birth of Jesus came to bring glad tidings of great joy to all peoples. (Luke 2:10). Romans, chapter 5 verse 18, states 'Therefore as by the offence of one judgement came upon all men to condemnation, even so by the righteousness of One the free gift came upon all men to justification of life.'

John, in his first epistle, chapter 2 verse 2, states, 'He is the propitiation for our sins and not for ours only, but also for the sins of the whole world.' Isaiah, chapter 53 verse 6, states, 'All we like sheep have gone astray and the Lord hath laid on Him the iniquity of us all.'

And this is far from teaching universalism, that in the end everyone will be saved. For that too would be contrary to Scripture and contrary to the free will of man, as it teaches that men are saved whether or not they believe. But it does teach that salvation is on offer to all.

The one thread which runs through all of Scripture as applying to those who are chosen or elected is 'believing'. Scripture clearly teaches that no one is saved by good works of any kind. For by grace are ye saved through faith and that not of yourselves; it is the gift of God; not of works lest any man should boast. (Ephesians 2:8-9).

That means, when Billy Graham says he knows he is going to Heaven, he is not, nor is any Christian, boasting that he is better than other people. He is saying that God offered him eternal life in Jesus, and he believed God and accepted the gift. If he had not believed, he would have made God a liar. 'He that believeth on the Son of God hath the witness in himself: he that believeth not God hath made Him a liar; because he believeth not the record that God gave of His Son.' (1 John 5:10).

Who ever when offered a gift would say, 'let me pay you for it'? We may have less gratitude for gifts than we ought as it is our custom to return gift for gift; but what gift could we give in exchange for an eternity in glory? We who could never afford to live in an earthly palace, how calmly we contemplate paying our way into a heavenly one.

How cheaply we evaluate the gift of eternal life and how highly we evaluate our own self-righteousness. And how lightly we contemplate the sinless Son of God hanging on the cross because of our sin: the love of God Who gave Him for us and the holiness of the God Who demanded such a sacrifice in His hatred of sin.

It may seem strange that all people do not hurry to receive this free gift of eternal life. It is the God-breathed spirit in man which feels the need of forgiveness and responds to the prompting of the Holy Spirit. It is evident all around that when the flesh is comfortable and enjoying itself, the spirit is quenched. Men feel immortal and in no need of thinking about life after death.

Some feel a stirring of the spirit and delude themselves they can have the best of both worlds by deciding themselves how they can worship and at the same time keep their independence.

These are those who produced their good works as self-justification, and to whom the Judge said 'Depart from Me, I never knew you' (Matthew 7:21-23).

Men confuse Biblical teaching about rewards when

they suppose the reward is eternal life; whereas eternal life, or salvation, is never a reward, but always a gift. The rewards for faithful service only come after the gift has been received and the only way to possess a gift is to accept it.

It is remarkable how we humans imagine we can ever offer anything to God which will enrich Him. We would have no existence if He had not created us.

We offer alms and money, but it is He who has given us power to get wealth (Deuteronomy 8:18). We offer good deeds and service but it is He Who has given us the talents, the health, the ability to serve. (1 Chronicles 29:14).

Nothing good which we do ever wipes out the wrongdoing, the lack of love to our fellow men and women, for when we are doing our good deeds and giving of our substance to church and charity, we are merely doing what it is our duty to do anyway, if we claim to belong to the family of God.

We don't particularly like the words of Jesus in Luke ch. 17 verse 10: 'When ye shall have done all these things which are commanded you say, We are unprofitable servants and we have done that which was our duty to do.'

No way can we sinful creatures exceed the goodness which is demanded of us in order to make up for the sins and shortcomings; not necessarily gross sins, just the love of self and of going our own way.

Only when we acknowledge that trying to save ourselves is like trying to lift ourselves by our own shoelaces, will we see that believing in, and surrender to, the One Who died to save us is the only way to receive eternal life.

Yes. Even 'believing' or 'faith' is the gift of God. We could have no capacity to believe if His Holy Spirit had not always been at work in the world, speaking to the hearts of men, drawing them to Himself. The initiative has always been His.

Surely that is why the gospel is to be preached to all the world, to all mankind. The prayer, 'Lord I believe, help Thou mine unbelief,' will never go unanswered.

Jesus has declared, 'If any man willeth to do His will he shall know of the doctrine whether it be of God.' (John 7:17) The response of the heart to the invitation to 'Come' and to believe is what is important. God is willing that all should be saved and come to the knowledge of the truth, (1 Timothy 2:4) therefore He is willing to accept all who respond by believing.

Paul's teaching in Romans, chapter 4, clearly differentiates between believing and works. 'For if Abraham were justified by works, he hath whereof to glory, but not before God. For what saith the Scriptures? Abraham believed God and it was reckoned unto him for righteousness'.

Reckoned by Whom? Not by man! Reckoned by God for righteousness. We could believe to the utmost but if God did not account belief for righteousness we would remain in our sin.

'Now to him that worketh is the reward not reckoned of grace but of debt. But to him that worketh not but believeth on Him that justifieth the ungodly his faith is reckoned for righteousness. (Romans 4:2-5).

In Romans, chapter 3 verse 22, Paul states, 'Even the righteousness of God which is through faith in Jesus Christ unto all and upon all them that believe'; and in verse 26, 'that He might be just and the justifier of him which believeth in Jesus'.

But our greatest argument of course comes from the lips of Jesus Himself. 'For God so loved the world that He gave His only-begotten Son that whosoever believeth on Him should not perish but have everlasting life'. (John 3:16) And from the invitation, 'Let him that is athirst come, and whosoever will, let him take the water of life freely' (Revelation 22:17); and further words from Jesus, 'This is the will of Him that sent Me that everyone which seeth the Son, and believeth on Him may have everlasting life.' (John 6:40).

When thought is given to the sin of Adam and Eve, it was not when they ate the forbidden fruit that they first sinned. Sin was already conceived when they decided in their hearts that God had not really meant it when He told them they would surely die. Their sin was unbelief. Unbelief led them to disobey. God has said we will die if we disobey him. We don't believe a word of it. We imagine we can pit ourselves against the Creator and find eternal life on our own terms.

So, Scripture shows that God's choosing and election were according to His foreknowledge of who would believe - not of who would do good works. And it is not even that believing would save us if He ordained otherwise, so His sovereignty is not affected. But He has ordained that those who respond to Him in belief and have faith in Him are chosen.

This does not mean believing about, but believing in; trusting and obeying; surrendering ourselves to Him, believing that we are totally bankrupt before Him and that we have done nothing to deserve His free gift of salvation.

Believing about Hitler did not make a Nazi Gestapo. Believing in Hitler, following and obeying him as Fuhrer, did. Believing about God and Jesus Christ does not make a Christian. Believing in Him, following and obeying Him as Lord and Saviour, does. Surrendering to the Lordship of Christ and trusting Him and the Father Who sent Him; believing His Word - all of it, not just the parts that we agree with, but all of it, and allowing it to speak the truth to our hearts.

To those who think they deserve salvation because they believe about the existence of God, James says in chapter 2 verse 19, 'Thou believest that there is one God; thou doest well. The devils also believe and tremble.' The devils believe about Him, but they are doomed.

Jesus told a parable of a certain man having two debtors - the one owed him fifty pence, and the other five hundred, but as they had nothing to pay him back, he frankly forgave them both. (Luke 7:41-42). It can hardly be called a merit to accept a receipt for the debt being wiped out. Who could say the two debtors contributed to the payment of their debt by believing the creditor when he said he forgave them all?

And so, for men and women to acknowledge their bankruptcy and, in deep gratitude for the mercy shown, to believe that the death of Jesus Messiah on the cross has undeservedly covered their sins, can hardly be termed participating in their own salvation, or paying for it in any way.

It is told of Augustus M. Toplady that it was the experience of seeking refuge from a storm, in a cleft of a rocky cliff, which inspired him to write 'Rock of Ages cleft for me'. I'm sure he never thought there was merit in seeking refuge in the Rock of Ages. Christ has created the shelter and calls us in from the storms of sin. If He had not provided the cleft we would be helpless. So in no way is His sovereignty affected by our obeying His call.

Because God in His sovereignty has created all things and in His sovereignty has dictated what is acceptable to Him, there is no way anything we can do can enrich Him or atone for our sinfulness.

Without the prompting and influence of His Holy Spirit we could not respond to the initiative which is His. There is

45

no merit in our responding in belief to His love, and those who believe are those whom He chooses.

The same Holy Spirit is working in this age of grace to seek to draw many who turn away and go their own way - responding in unbelief to the certainty that there will be damnation resulting from their choice. Not because God sends them to Hell. He has done all that is necessary to save them from Hell; but because they choose the road that leads there, either ignoring the warnings, or imagining that they can step off that road at the last minute of life, when they have eaten their cake and had their good time.

CHAPTER X

....and He shall execute judgement in the Land. (Jeremiah 33:15).

Those who hold that believing is somehow participating in our own salvation, and that God choses whom He wills for no known reason, say also that God can do anything He likes and it is sinful to question His justice.

Well! Praise His Holy Name, the things He likes to do are just. He has the power to do anything. But He has chosen not to do those things which are contrary to His Nature. He has power to lie, to break promises, to change, but He does none of those things.

His word teaches us that He is long-suffering and not willing that any should perish but that all should come to repentance (2 Peter 3:9). That being so, if God chose some to salvation with no reference to their believing, it would seem that the best way He could have given Himself pleasure would have been to destroy Satan and choose all for salvation.

So why did He not? There is much mystery here. How much pain and horrors would never have been if all were chosen to life. But it would seem that the Lord desired a people who would respond to Him despite pain, a people who would believe Him and repent of the times they have hurt and disobeyed Him. A people chosen in the furnace of affliction, (Isaiah 48:10).

Not a people who could do no other than obey Him, because they were elected to be believers. A people of whom He could truly say to Satan, 'See My servants who have loved Me in spite of all you could do to them; who have believed

Me and accepted My strength to help them overcome.'

The foreknowledge of which Scripture speaks, was not of good works, but of who would believe, and because His desire was for a people who would love Him freely, and respond to Him freely, for the initiative is always with Him. 'Ye have not chosen Me but I have chosen you.' (John 15:16). Of course He has chosen us if we were chosen in Him before the foundation of the world.

Those who maintain that God can, in His sovereignty, send us all into oblivion if He so chose, so we undeserving sinners should not question His justice, forget one thing. On the cross, His Son bought us. His shed blood paid the price for our redemption and justice was satisfied.

This is one instance where God has the power to change His mind about His creation, but cannot in His own justice do so. He has promised His salvation to those who believe and cannot break His promise. If He did He would not be the God revealed in the Bible.

Praise Him forever that there are things He cannot do and remain true to Himself. It is that very stability which give us assurance.

There was a time when the children of Israel questioned His justice. They had a proverb - 'The Fathers have eaten sour grapes and the children's teeth are set on edge,' implying they were being punished for the sins of their fathers. God could have sent them His word through Ezekiel (Chs. 18 & 33) that He was sovereign and could do as He pleased and they would just have to accept it.

But far from doing that, He is angry that He should have been accused of injustice, and shows how His ways are 'equal'. In both chapters, God declares He has no pleasure in the death of the wicked, but rather that the wicked should turn from his ways and live.

Before that, in chapter 14 verse 23, God promises a remnant of comfort following His retribution. He declares 'And ye shall know that I have not done without cause all that I have done saith the Lord.' He wants us to be sure that His ways are always just and that there is always a reason for judgement. In fact His Word is shot through with His teaching on justice.

And far from not wanting us to question His ways, including His justice, He has constantly revealed that we should 'go on to know Him'. The most important thing we can do as we study His Word is to learn all we can of His nature and what He has revealed of Himself - to know Him.

Jesus in His prayer to His Father declared, 'And this is life eternal that they might know Thee the only true God, and Jesus Christ Whom Thou hast sent.' (John 17:3).

Peter's greeting was 'Grace and peace be multiplied unto you through the knowledge of God and of Jesus our Lord according as His divine power hath given us all things that pertain to life and godliness through the knowledge of Him that hath called us to glory and virtue..' (2 Peter 1:2).

Jeremiah, ch. 9 verse 24, states, 'Let him that glorieth, glory in this that he understandeth and knoweth Me, that I am the Lord which exercise loving kindness, judgement and righteousness in the earth, for in these things I delight saith the Lord.'. So much for the 'cruel God' of the Old Testament!

We are all aware that there are degrees of knowing a person; from the stranger who recognizes a face to the relation and close friend. Those who commute to work each day with the same group of people would say they know one another, though they may never exchange opinions or views on anything other than the weather, or the state of the economy or the latest sports results.

People who live in the same household will have a more personal knowledge of each other as regards likes and dislikes and temperament, but even here there is often a lack of communication about anything other than the surface things of daily living.

Colleagues at work will have an idea of each others' abilities and temperaments but may have not the least conception of each others' private lives or home background.

All these would say they know each other, but it is only a surface knowing. It is only when people are close to each other, interested in each other, sharing ideas and ambitions, problems and sorrows, joys and victories, that they can truly say they know each other.

How relevant it can be to know if you can trust another person. If you are walking through a lonely park after dark you may be nervous as a figure approaches until he passes under a light and you recognize a trusted friend - all fear vanishes.

Or would you approach a person you know to be mean about money if you were collecting for a good cause? Or confide in someone you knew to be a gossip?

And so in knowing God. The more we get to know Him the more we have confidence that what we ask for is in accordance with His will, and the more we can trust Him to keep us at all times.

Is it right to say we do not know why God chooses some when He has revealed so much about His ways? He calls those who are obedient to Him friends (John 15:14-15). Masters do not always confide in their servants but friends exchange confidences and understand each other.

Though we can never in this world, while in the flesh,

understand God perfectly, we can always, if we have a desire to know and to search for an answer, have a good idea why He has acted in a certain manner.

There is an interesting case of David being 'displeased' by God's action. It was when he had been confirmed as king following the death of Saul. He desired to bring the Ark of the Covenant from Kirjath-Jearim 'home to himself' and had gathered the congregation of Israel together to make it a great event.

They carried the ark in a new cart and Uzziah and Ahio drove the cart which was pulled by oxen. When the oxen stumbled Uzziah put out his hand to hold the ark to steady it, and we are told 'the anger of the Lord was kindled against Uzziah and He smote him because he put his hand to the Ark and there he died before God.' 'And David was displeased because the Lord made a breach upon Uzziah.' In other words David questioned God's justice. 'And David was afraid of God that day, and did not bring the ark any further but left it nearby'. (1 Chronicles 13).

Shortly after we find David has obviously thought long and hard about the Lord's action and had humbly sought an answer. He learned the great lesson that God will only be worshipped in the way He has ordained and not just as men please.

The heathen carried their idols around in carts at festivals (Isaiah 46:1-2), but Jehovah had said the ark of the Covenant was to be carried by staves on the shoulders of Levites consecrated to that office. When David again proposed to bring the ark of the Covenant home, he prepared a tent for it and admitted that 'none ought to carry the Ark of God but the Levites, for them hath the Lord chosen to carry the ark of God and to minister to Him for ever.' (1 Chronicles 15:2). And

51

verse 13, 'because ye did it not at the first the Lord our God made a breach upon us for that we sought Him not after the due order.' And so 'the children of the Levites bare the Ark of God upon their shoulders with the staves thereon as Moses commanded according to the Word of the Lord.'

From this we see that God sometimes has to use very sore measures to remind us that He is sovereign, and is not to be approached lightly or thoughtlessly. And we see that God revealed the reason for His action, and was not offended by David's questioning the reason.

To return to our thoughts on knowing God. Many believe God exists but He has no relevance to their every-day lives. Others give Him a place on Sundays and contribute to His church, but they have no intention of letting Him intrude into their way of living, their worldly pleasures, where they go or what they do.

Sadly there is also a large group in His church who profess that they belong to Him and who are involved in committees and social activities connected with the church. They have come to a knowledge of God's salvation but after that they have no desire to follow on to know Him better.

They are content to have got their foot in the door so to speak, but there is no longing to read His Word. If the choice were between a social or sports outing or a T.V. programme, and the Bible class or prayer meeting, pleasure would win the day and they see little pleasure in the Bible class or in private study of God's Word. As Jeremiah, chapter 6 verse 10, states, they have 'no delight in the Word of the Lord'.

What a sad thing it is that there is so little desire to know God even among many church members, those who are called by His Name. What a wealth of knowledge and delight they miss by being content to paddle in the shallows, or to use

Paul's expression, to feed on milk instead of solid food; milk which is the nourishment of babies, but not of adults except they be very sick.

But the day will come when they will say, 'that which has not been told us has come to pass'. They will know that Israel went into captivity because of her rejection of God, and He will be sanctified in Israel before the eyes of the world when all that His Word has foretold has come to pass.

In that day no doubt, men and women will be leafing through their Bibles in an effort to know more, but how sad there is so little desire to know Him now, to know what pleases Him, to know what He would have them do to further His Kingdom in the world.

CHAPTER XI

Hath not the potter power over the clay of the same lump to make one vessel unto honour and another unto dishonour? (Romans 9:21).

So! before the foundation of the world God chose those who would believe with reference to personal salvation. 'Whosoever believeth on Him shall not be ashamed.' (Romans 9:33). Where election branches out now, is in the matter of it being completely a matter of God's choice in what capacity each would serve His purpose.

God chose those who would believe, and out of this conglomerate of believers and unbelievers, He worked out a plan of action in order to bring about His eternal purpose in creating the world. He elected the capacity in which each created being would serve His purpose and this without reference to any will but His own.

The all-seeing all-wise Creator is the only One Who can bring about the circumstances and conditions in which He will be sanctified in the eyes of all creation. He elected Abraham to be the founder of His chosen nation. He elected Isaac to inherit the promises rather than Ishmael, and Jacob rather than Esau. He elected Joseph to save the seedling nation in time of famine. He elected Moses to lead the growing nation which had fallen into bondage, out of that bondage, into a Land of Promise, and to be His law-giver. He elected Mary to be the mother of His Son when the time came for Him to be made flesh. He elected apostles to be an inner circle of followers, to learn His gospel, and proclaim it to the world, and He elected Paul to interpret that gospel, which he had been taught by the Holy Spirit, and to pass it on to generations to come, and to all the peoples of the earth, leading them to belief and faith in Messiah.

This does not detract from man's freedom, as those who believe Him have yielded themselves wholly to His disposal. To some He will say 'Go', 'Go to those people and tell', to others 'Go home and tell'.

Some will be teachers, some missionaries. For each and every child of His, He has a purpose - as the hymn puts it, 'There's a work for Jesus none but you can do.'

As Ephesians, chapter 2 verse 10, states, 'We are His workmanship created in Christ Jesus unto good works which God has before ordained that we should walk in them.'

As it is God's will that all men should be saved, it is obvious that all cannot be evangelists, or all teachers or preachers, but that He ordains many to just be a christian society; business people; professional and lay; white and blue collar workers; butchers, bakers, candlestick makers. Some with many natural talents in high places and some with the also very necessary serving talents. Some to marriage and family life; some who can only carry out His purpose by remaining single.

As God foreknew who would believe, so He foreknew who would reject. He did not ordain their rejection, but through the preaching of prophets and evangelists has offered a salvation which is available to all. As these owe the very breath of life to Him, it is no injustice that He can use them also, in whatever capacity, to be sanctified in them and to further His purposes in the world.

There is much that happens in the world which is contrary to His will. You cannot say it is His will that children should be abused, and that mankind should indulge in gross sins, when you know He has expressly forbidden such things in His Word.

Yet such things do not hinder His eternal purposes, nor ever get beyond His control. Nor will the sometimes disobedience of His own children who do not follow His plain guidance change His inexorable purposes for the world. He has appointed a time when He will pour out retribution on those who continue in evil ways, and who, under Satan's dominion, try to frustrate His good and perfect will.

Scripture is clear that there will be a day of reckoning for all, when we are called to give an account of the deeds done in the flesh. (Romans 14:12).

He has chosen, and as Creator He has every right to choose, the nation of Israel, to be sanctified in them before the nations of the world. 'Thou art My servant O Israel in whom I will be glorified.' (Isaiah 49:3).

In His infinite knowledge and wisdom He is working His purposes out in the world. He has spoken through His prophets and made plain His choice of Israel, and His judgement on all the nations who oppose her - for those who oppose her, oppose His will. Isaiah states, 'Thus saith the Lord, even the captives of the mighty shall be taken away and the prey of the terrible shall be delivered, for I will contend with him that contendeth with thee and I will save thy children. And I will feed them that oppress thee with their own flesh.... and all flesh shall know that I the Lord am thy Saviour and thy Redeemer, the mighty One of Jacob.' (49:25-26).

Chapter 54 verse 15 states, 'Whosoever shall gather together against thee shall fall for thy sake.' Verse 17: 'No weapon that is formed against thee shall prosper and every tongue that shall rise against thee in judgement thou shalt condemn. This is the heritage of the servants of the Lord and their righteousness is of Me saith the Lord.'

Does anyone imagine that it was the military might of

Britain which overcame Germany and Italy in the Second World War? She started the war with next to no military equipment and a very weak defence machine. In the providence of God Hitler did not invade Britain and believers see the over-ruling hand of God working out His judgement and retribution on those who had tortured and cruelly treated His own people, the Jews.

Believers see it because He has made it so plain in His Word. Fewer and fewer will see it in these days when there is such an abysmal ignorance of even the most basic facts in the Bible. One only has to watch some Quiz Shows on Television to know that!

CHAPTER XII

For it is the day of the Lord's vengeance and the year of recompense for the controversy of Zion. (Isaiah 34:8).

Some believers may throw up their hands in horror at the idea that God sends retribution on nations, but Scripture shows clearly that He does.

Jeremiah states, 'And many nations shall pass by this city and they shall say every man to his neighbour, Wherefore hath the Lord done thus unto this great city? Then they shall answer, Because they have forsaken the covenant of the Lord their God, and worshipped other gods and served them.' (22:8-9).

This is not an isolated case as over fifty times in this Book are similar declarations showing 'Because they..... therefore I.'

The Book of Ezekiel shows over fifty times that, because of the way the Lord brings retribution on one or another nation, 'Then shall they know that I AM the Lord.'

And if the argument is that these instances are from the Old Testament, then read the Book of Revelation in the New Testament to know what Heaven pours out on the earth, and read the forecasts which Jesus made of the 'end times'. I'm afraid as in Jeremiah's day, many preachers 'say still unto them that despise Me, The Lord hath said, ye shall have peace; and they say unto every one that walketh after the imagination of his own heart, No evil shall come upon you.' (Jeremiah 23:17).

When finally God's purposes have been brought to a climax then the whole world will acknowledge His choosing of Israel to be a special people to Himself - they shall call them 'the holy people; the redeemed of the Lord' (Isaiah 62:12).

'Then the nations that are round about you shall know that I the Lord build the ruined places.' (Ezekiel 36:36). 'The heathen shall know that I the Lord do sanctify Israel when My Sanctuary shall be in the midst of them forever more.' (Ezekiel 37:28).

'The heathen shall know that I AM the Lord the Holy One of Israel.' (Ezekiel 39:7), and verse 23, 'the heathen shall know that the House Of Israel went into captivity for their iniquity.'

The evidence that God's covenant with Abraham was an everlasting covenant, that He has never fully cast off Abraham's 'seed', but is still working out His purposes, and fulfilling His Word, through Israel, is overwhelming. But only overwhelming to those who search the Scriptures; who have complete confidence in God's Word, because they know the One Who speaks it, and are persuaded that 'He is faithful that promised.'

It would be impossible not to believe that God takes sides on behalf of Israel, when He is working out His elected purposes in choosing her. That is, unless we are to discount all that we do not agree with and only leave the Scriptures which please us.

But the Canon of Scripture is that which judges us; not that which we pick and choose to agree with. We would have to cut out the many instances of God's intervention against the enemies who threatened Israel's existence and it would be a very anaemic Book which was left.

In Judges (chapter 7) we are told of Gideon's strategy against the Midianites when the Lord had reduced Gideon's army to three hundred men. But verse 22 states 'The Lord set every man's sword against his fellow even throughout all the host.' The result? Israel's enemies were defeated.

We would lose the inspiring story of Saul's son Jonathan's faith when fighting the enemy. We are told in 1 Samuel, chapter 14 verse 6, that he said to his armour bearer, 'It may be that the Lord will work for there is no restraint to the Lord to save by many or by few.' And his faith was vindicated for 'the multitude melted away and they went on beating one another down.' (v.16) Why? 'Because every man's sword was against his fellow.' (v.20).

Good king Jehoshaphat was told, when confronted by the enemy, 'Be not afraid nor dismayed by reason of this great multitude for the battle is not yours but God's. Ye shall not need to fight in this battle. Set yourselves, stand ye still and see the salvation of the Lord; fear not nor be dismayed.... tomorrow go out against them for the Lord will be with you ... And when they began to sing and to praise, the Lord set ambushments against the children of Ammon, Moab and Mount Seir which were come against Judah, and they were smitten. For the children of Ammon and Moab stood up against the inhabitants of Mount Seir utterly to slay and destroy them and when they had made an end of the inhabitants of Seir everyone helped to destroy another... And when Judah came towards the Watch Tower in the wilderness, they looked unto the multitude and behold they were all dead bodies fallen to the earth and none escaped.' (2 Chronicles 20:15-24).

We must never believe that God has changed and that these stories were accounted for by the notion that men did not know God's true nature and were mistaken in their beliefs.

Remember that Jesus claimed to be the I AM of the Old Testament when He declared 'Before Abraham was, I AM.' (John 8:58). The Old Testament is replete with instances of the grace, love and loving kindness of Jehovah. The New Testament shows us that same Jehovah voluntarily taking flesh to die for the redemption of the world. And also warning of judgement to come, and of punishment for disobedience. Read Matthew (chapter 23) to know the woes He expresses upon those who reject Him, called by Him 'serpents, ye generation of vipers, how can ye escape the damnation of hell?' (v.33).

CHAPTER XIII

.... and ye shall be witnesses unto Me both in Jerusalem and in all Judea and in Samaria and unto the uttermost part of the earth. (Acts 1:8).

It is quite right that there should be a good relationship between Jew and Gentile, with each respecting the other's beliefs. In a democratic and free society there should be room to be able to express those beliefs and to try to persuade others of the truth as one sees it.

That is why members of various cults are free to go from door to door, to engage the home occupants in conversation about their doctrines. All that those who object have to do, is to gently close the door. That is one of the privileges of a civilized society; there being no need to start a riot to protest.

Those who are sure of the grounds of their own faith have nothing to fear in discussion with those who differ. But unfortunately there have been those down the years who thought they were doing God's will in persecuting the Jews.

Although Jesus had told Peter to put away his sword on the night that Jesus was betrayed, there have been those who called themselves by Christ's Name who have taken up the sword to persecute and hound Jews and who have sought to exterminate them as a people. They have made the lovely Name of Jesus Christ to be abhorred.

To call a Jew 'Christ killer' is a travesty of the truth, and springs from complete ignorance of God's plan of salvation for the world. Apart from the fact that, humanly speaking, the issue of life or death for Jesus lay in Roman hands, when Pilate avowed he had power to crucify and power to release Jesus (John 19:10); and it was Roman hands which drove in the nails; yet Jesus had said, 'No man taketh My Life from Me - I lay it down of Myself.' (John 10:17-18). When Christ died, He died for the sins of the world, Jew and Gentile. Every human being from Adam and Eve to the last man and woman on earth is a 'Christ killer'.

Of course, in the early days of the church, it was the other way round; it was the Jewish leaders who persecuted the followers of Jesus, and those were their fellow Jews. It just happens that in the matter of religious beliefs there is very little tolerance towards those who differ. And this is true today as in the dark ages past.

The present resentment against evangelizing unbelievers in Jesus, be they Jew or Gentile, follows the same pattern as in the days of the apostles, with protests and false accusations. But, as Peter declared when challenged about teaching in 'this Name', 'We ought to obey God rather than men (Acts 5:29). Of Jesus Peter said 'Him hath God exalted with His right hand to be a Prince and a Saviour for to give repentance to Israel and forgiveness of sins.'

When the apostles had been imprisoned, 'the angel of the Lord by night opened the prison doors and brought them forth.' 'Go stand and speak in the Temple to the people all the words of this life' they were told. The Jewish Temple of course. (Acts 5:19-20).

When later Paul had his conversion experience on the road to Damascus and was temporarily blinded, Ananias was told in a vision to go to him and restore his sight. Protesting that Paul was a persecutor of the church, Ananias was told, 'Go thy way for he (Paul) is a chosen vessel unto Me to bear My Name before the Gentiles and kings, and the children of

Israel.' And immediately afterwards Paul 'preached Christ in the Synagogues that He is the Son of God.' (Acts 9:15,20).

And of course the great commission of Jesus to His disciples before He ascended to His Father was, 'that repentance and remission of sins should be preached in His Name among all nations beginning at Jerusalem.' (Luke 24:47).

Just as in the days of the apostles, we have to obey God rather than men for His commission still stands. That we should refrain from presenting Jesus to His own (John 1:11) is unthinkable and would constitute dereliction of duty and disobedience to Him.

Far from the special relationship (which the Bible teaches God has with the nation of Israel) being a reason for not evangelizing the Jews, it should be a reason for making every effort to persuade them that Jesus is their promised Messiah.

It can hardly be supposed that because a person is a descendant of Abraham, through Isaac and Jacob, he or she is automatically the recipient of eternal life. There have been many wicked and idolatrous children of Abraham, as the Bible clearly demonstrates, not least Judas Iscariot - as judged by Jesus, 'Woe to that man by whom the Son of Man is betrayed. It had been good for that man if he had not been born. (Matthew 26:24).

The Bible clearly teaches that 'all have sinned and come short of the glory of God, being justified freely by His grace through the redemption that is in Christ Jesus' (Romans 3:23-24). It is very hard to understand how someone who claims to be a Christian can, in the name of friendship for Jews and from a desire not to offend, be antagonistic to those who proclaim the way of salvation to Jews.

It would be interesting to know on what basis they themselves came to Christ and what is their assessment of Him who declared 'No one cometh unto the Father but by Me.' (John 14:6). That very claim is an offence to Gentiles as well as to the Jews, but we do not therefore close down all mission stations and stop the churches reaching out to evangelize.

The truth is that true friendship to the sons of Abraham is to make every effort to introduce Jesus their Messiah to them, and thereby hasten the day when they as a nation will say, 'Blessed is He that cometh in the Name of the Lord.' What a day that will be, and it is surely, but surely, coming. (Matthew 23:39).

There have been many Jews who converted to Christianity and assimilated with the Gentile church, turning their backs on past customs and traditions. But in these days many find that far from losing their Jewish identity, and far from it being impossible to be a Jew and a Christian, They are fulfilled Jews who have found their Messiah. Just as the various nations have their ethos of worship, so these Jewish believers have a recognisable form of Jewish worship, and have lost nothing of their Jewishness, and lost nothing of their love for their nation and its traditions.

These are still the first-fruits and a tiny trickle of what will be a torrent of believers in Yeshua ha Meshiach, when the nation of Israel look on Him Whom they have pierced and realize the sin of their long rejection of Him. 'And it shall come to pass in that day that I will seek to destroy all the nations that come against Jerusalem. And I will pour upon the house of David, and upon the inhabitants of Jerusalem, the spirit of grace and of supplications, and they shall look upon Me Whom they have pierced...' (Zechariah 12:10).

And some say we should keep the truth of Messiah

from them and delay rather than expedite the day for which the nation was created. For shame!

CHAPTER XIV

And the Lord said unto Satan, 'Behold he is in thine hand; but save his life.' (Job 2:6).

It may seem as though there is injustice in God's punishment of the whole nation when it would seem it was the leaders only who rejected Jesus as Messiah, and even of them some believed.

There were those who, after the miraculous feeding of the multitude wanted to make Jesus King. But Jesus knew their hearts (John 2:25) and was not flattered, but rebuked them. 'Ye seek Me, not because ye saw the miracles, but because ye did eat of the loaves and were filled. Labour not for the meat that perisheth but for that meat which endureth unto life everlasting which the Son of Man shall give unto you.' (John 6:26,27).

After having seen the miracle they could say to Him, 'What sign showest Thou then that we may see and believe Thee?' What's so wonderful about feeding thousands? Moses did the same and he was not Messiah.

When Jesus had reasoned with them they found the spiritual teaching too much for them and 'many of His disciples went back and walked no more with Him.' And Jesus was left with His 'remnant' of twelve - and one of them would betray Him. (John 6:66).

There were others who believed Him, like Lazarus and his sisters Mary and Martha, and the women who ministered to Him; the man who let Him have his young foal to ride into Jerusalem; the owner of the room where the last supper was prepared.

But three years of teaching, preaching, healing and living a perfect life of love and service did not bring about a revival, nor a spirit of repentance among the people. They had no desire to 'walk with Him', but were, in Jesus' estimation, 'a faithless and perverse generation'. (Matthew 17:17).

We are told in John (chapter 12 verse 36) that, 'Jesus departed and did hide Himself from them.' He saw clearly, He Who knew what was in man, that though He had done so many miracles before them, yet they believed not on Him.

So in fact God reciprocated their treatment of Messiah and walked no more with *them*. And with His withdrawal went the ability to see and understand the truths of Scripture and of the gospel. A veil came down over their spiritual eyes.

There can be no complaint about God's justice in this. They had made their choice to reject the truth, to reject their Messiah; so Truth left them.

There are some who say that love is blind. But it is surely more true to say that hatred is blind. And nothing would illustrate this more than Satan's hatred of the Jews.

Good law-abiding citizens in the countries to which they have been scattered, they have contributed much to the culture and prosperity of those countries where they have settled - in music, science, learning and other ways. And as of yore in Biblical history they have wanted to be like those around them and to be assimilated.

Yet time and again, even when they have been born and bred in a country, they have been singled out for rejection and persecution, and for no logical reason. Nothing could explain it but the blind hatred of Satanic powers.

If hatred had not blinded Satan's eyes he would have

known that the best way to have got rid of these 'favourites' of his old Enemy, the Almighty Creator, would have been to leave them in peace and let them assimilate and gradually be indistinguishable from the rest of humanity.

Surely God allowed this singling out of His people as the way He was going to preserve them down through the 2000 years when they were without a country or government of their own. No one can deny the miracle of their survival as a distinct people.

God's punishment was to dispossess them of His Land and withdraw His special protection - 'How oft would I.... but ye would not! ....and now your House is left unto you desolate.'

But always, as in the case of Job, He sets limits beyond which Satan cannot go. He was preserving His Remnant through whom He would yet be sanctified in the sight of the nations, and He has never forgotten His covenant promises to Abraham, Isaac and Jacob.

And God has stated that though He has punished Israel for her sins and allowed nations to treat her shamefully yet He will bring punishment on those who oppressed her. Jeremiah (chapter 30 verse 16) states, 'Therefore all they that devour thee shall be devoured and all thine adversaries every one of them shall go into captivity and they that spoil thee shall be a spoil and all that prey upon thee will I give for a prey.' Verse 20: 'I will punish all that oppress them.' Verse 24: '..in the latter days ye shall consider it.'

In Isaiah (chapter 51 verse 22) the Lord states 'Behold I have taken out of thine hand the cup of trembling, even the dregs of the cup of My fury'; He states, in verse 23, 'But I will put it into the hand of them that afflict thee, which have said to thy soul, Bow down that we may go over thee; and thou hast laid thy body as the ground and as the street to them that went over.'

CHAPTER XV

The wilderness and the solitary place shall be glad and the desert shall rejoice and blossom as the rose. It shall blossom abundantly and rejoice even with joy and singing. (Isaiah 35:1-2).

It was only right and just that a people who were singled out for rejection by the nations, should be given land where they could govern themselves. And where else would that land be but their historical homeland?

It was not all given free. Much that was desert and marshland was sold to Jews by absentee Arab landlords who had done nothing with all their wealth to improve the land, or the standard of living of their Arab tenants. They thought they were being paid for worthless land, but hard work and ingenuity, and much sacrifice by the new Jewish owners, caused the land to blossom and flourish.

It was inevitable that many Arabs would object to the land being reoccupied by its ancient citizens, and wars were the result. As the Arab nations united to attack Israel in attempts to recover the land and dispossess the Jews, they lost even more land.

They present a picture of a once-rich Arab standing on the steps of a Casino weeping and calling out that he wants his money back. Can anyone imagine that passers-by would have sympathy for him and back him up in his demand?

Yet that is precisely what the world is doing in supporting Arab claims to have their land restored. They gambled and lost and then wanted everything back again. Does anyone imagine if they had over-run Israel that they would have withdrawn at the world's behest?

70

When we look at a map of the Middle East we see the vast expanses of land and yet there is so much fuss about this little strip given to a persecuted people. What, other than Satanic hatred, could inspire such reaction?

If the Jewish people had been given a similar strip in the middle of the Sahara Desert, there would have been the same enmity and persecution, especially when the Arabs saw that desert blossoming and becoming fertile, as it most assuredly would.

And what other than the Lord's protection could have given such overwhelming victory to Israeli forces against the combined Arab attacks?

And He will always give them victory until they possess all of the land promised to their forefathers.

It is sad that some sections of the Christian church support the Arab cause against Israel. Can anyone recall the churches taking up the cause of Arab poverty against rich Arab landowners? And nothing is heard of Israel's offer to build homes for the refugees which was turned down as the living conditions make too good a propaganda picture, for the rest of the world to turn against Israel.

Surely neglect of the Old Testament is largely the reason for feelings of enmity against Israel. Many hear portions of Scripture read only when they attend church. The Higher criticism which many ministers were taught in colleges has weakened their faith in the trustworthiness of the Old Testament.

Now, later archeological finds have proved much of that criticism to have been purely speculative and unfounded, but the damage has been done. Much biblical criticism, based on so-called science, was made by men who refused to believe in the divine revelation of future events. 'Impossible,' they said, 'to see into the future'. And so when events came to pass as predicted they had to explain them as having been recorded after the events took place. Some science.

According to that reasoning the return of the Jews to the Land of Israel has not yet been written. But the truth is it was predicted thousands of years ago. And the Bible records stand vindicated - with an exactitude which would almost seem to be recorded after the fulfilment of the prophecies.

Neglect of the study of the whole Bible means people are ignorant of the many promises and forecasts of blessing to this miraculously preserved nation.

Considering the number of quotations from the Old Testament in the New, it is surprising the New has survived. My Bible concordance lists almost 300 quotes from the Old Testament as well as over 200 references to statements and incidents. So if the Old Testament is not to be regarded as reliable, then the New Testament is built on sand and should have collapsed long ago.

But far from doing that, the Bible is still the world's best seller and has proved to be the Sword of the Spirit, penetrating to the very heart of its opponents in convicting and converting power.

People imagine the early apostles going out to evangelize with a New Testament in their hands, but in fact their way, under the influence of the Holy Spirit, was to show from the Old Testament how Jesus fulfilled the criteria to be the looked-for Messiah of Israel, and testifying to His death and resurrection as the remedy for sin for all the world.

Of course Scripture states, 'God so loved the world,' and of course He loves Arab people along with all the other nations of the world. As well as showing God's dealings and purposes for Israel, the Old Testament also speaks of His purposes for other nations.

Zechariah (chapter 2 verses 10 to 12) states, 'Sing and rejoice, O daughter of Zion; for, lo, I come, and I will dwell in the midst of thee, saith the Lord. And many nations shall be joined to the Lord in that day and shall be My people; and I will dwell in the midst of thee, and thou shalt know that the Lord of Hosts hath sent Me unto thee. And the Lord shall choose Jerusalem again.' Verse 9 of chapter 3 states, 'I will remove the iniquity of that land in one day.' We in our day have seen similar 'miracles' in one day, with the collapse of communism.

And Isaiah (chapter 19 verses 24 and 25) tells us, 'In that day shall Israel be the third with Egypt and with Assyria, even a blessing in the midst of the land. Whom the Lord of Hosts shall bless saying, Blessed be Egypt My people and Assyria the work of My hands, and Israel Mine inheritance.'

It is unfortunate that the nations of the world hate the Instrument God has chosen to fulfil His purposes in bringing many peoples to Himself. It will be to their own hurt to reject that Instrument, but the Bible is clear that the time is surely coming when they will acknowledge that they were wrong. They will 'take hold out of all languages of the nations, even shall take hold of the skirt of him that is a Jew, saying, 'We will go with you for we have heard that God is with you.' (Zechariah 8:23).

Hath God cast away His people? Never.

CHAPTER XVI

Ye men of Galilee, why stand ye gazing up into Heaven? this same Jesus which is taken up from you into Heaven shall so come in like manner as ye have seen Him go into Heaven. (Acts 1:11).

If it has been exciting to see the fulfilment of a promise made by God through His prophets thousands of years ago, it is sobering to remember that the fulfilment was to take place 'in the latter days'. In other words at the end of the age.

It has been very apparent to Christians that the conditions described by Jesus as heralding His return to earth are the conditions in which we are living today, and see daily on our television screens. Wars, famines of ghastly proportion, pestilences, natural disasters are seen by us all. (Matthew 24:7).

Would a Seer of old, gazing into the future in a trance-like dream, have seen the burning oil wells of Kuwait with smoke blotting out the sun and moon and stars; rivers of oil running into the sea to pollute and kill wild life? Television pictures of this certainly brought Bible predictions to mind.

These will happen on a much wider scale, but we who know of the speed with which events can overtake us, should be recognizing the imminence of the return of Jesus Messiah, not this time to a lowly stable but in triumphant glory to reign as King; to judge the living and the dead.

'When the Son of Man shall come in His glory and all the holy angels with Him, then shall He sit upon the throne of His glory. And before Him shall be gathered all nations, and He shall separate them one from another as a shepherd divideth his sheep from the goats.' (Matthew 25:31-32).

The Bible tells us He will reign from Mount Zion, from His holy city of Jerusalem. And conservationists take note. He is coming to 'destroy them which destroy the earth.' (Revelation 11:18).

The measure of our desire to see Him face to face should tell us how prepared we are for such an event. If we dread it, the 'day of the Lord' will be a black day for us.

But we are still living in the day of grace, and have an opportunity to accept His offer of eternal life; of acceptance by Him into His kingdom; and more, of adoption by Him into His family.

If we still put off the decision to believe Him, and to trust Him for salvation, then He has said He will come as a thief in the night, at a time when we are not looking for Him and then it will be too late.

Let us rather decide we want to know Him more fully, and to share in the blessings which we are promised along with His people Israel.

Let us offer ourselves to Him for the work He has for us to do in furthering His kingdom on earth. 'Ye are My friends if ye do whatsoever I command you.' Imagine the privilege of being a friend of the Lord of the Universe.

There is really no excuse for saying, 'Where are the signs of His coming? As things have been so they are.' (2 Peter 3:4). The signs are everywhere as study of God's Word will show.

So watch out for God's dealing with the nation of Israel and see His Word fulfilled. See and know that He has not cast off His people Whom He foreknew, but will yet be sanctified in them before the whole world.